aLpHa

PLANNER TRACKER

for all those in search
of life changing gains

BELONGS TO

____

____

aLpHa

PLANNER TRACKER

Trading Journal

Journal designed in the west coast.

CORE VALUES / GOALS

1. ______________________________

2. ______________________________

3. ______________________________

4. ______________________________

5. ______________________________

6. ______________________________

7. ______________________________

8. ______________________________

CALENDAR

Year :
Month :

NOTES

SUNDAY	MONDAY	TUESDAY

"Your days are numbered. Use them to throw open the windows of your soul to the sun. If you do not, the sun will soon set, and you with it." - Marcus Aurelius

WEDNESDAY	THURSDAY	FRIDAY	SATURDAY

CALENDAR

Year :
Month :

NOTES

SUNDAY	MONDAY	TUESDAY

"Before you can make a dream come true, you must first have one." - Ronald McNair

WEDNESDAY	THURSDAY	FRIDAY	SATURDAY

CALENDAR

Year :
Month :

NOTES

SUNDAY	MONDAY	TUESDAY

"The biggest risk of all is not taking one."
- Mellody Hobson

WEDNESDAY	THURSDAY	FRIDAY	SATURDAY

CALENDAR

Year :
Month :

NOTES

SUNDAY	MONDAY	TUESDAY

"Compound interest is the eighth wonder of the world. He who understands it, earns it. He who doesn't, pays it." - Albert Einstein

WEDNESDAY	THURSDAY	FRIDAY	SATURDAY

CALENDAR

Year :
Month :

NOTES

SUNDAY	MONDAY	TUESDAY

"If you don't fall, how are you going to know what getting up is like?" - Stephen Curry

WEDNESDAY	THURSDAY	FRIDAY	SATURDAY

CALENDAR

Year :
Month :

NOTES

SUNDAY	MONDAY	TUESDAY

"Don't look for the needle in the haystack. Just buy the haystack!" - John Bogle

WEDNESDAY	THURSDAY	FRIDAY	SATURDAY

CALENDAR

Year :
Month :

NOTES

SUNDAY	MONDAY	TUESDAY

"The wisest rule in investment is: when others are selling, buy. When others are buying, sell."
- Jonathan Sacks

WEDNESDAY	THURSDAY	FRIDAY	SATURDAY

CALENDAR

Year :
Month :

NOTES

SUNDAY	MONDAY	TUESDAY

"With a good perspective on history, we can have a better understanding of the past and present, and thus a clear vision of the future." - Carlos Slim Helu

WEDNESDAY	THURSDAY	FRIDAY	SATURDAY

CALENDAR

Year :
Month :

NOTES

SUNDAY	MONDAY	TUESDAY

"Divide your portion to seven, or even to eight, for you do not know what misfortune may occur on the earth." - King Solomon

WEDNESDAY	THURSDAY	FRIDAY	SATURDAY

CALENDAR

Year :
Month :

NOTES

SUNDAY	MONDAY	TUESDAY

"The stock market is filled with individuals who know the price of everything, but the value of nothing." - Phillip Fisher

WEDNESDAY	THURSDAY	FRIDAY	SATURDAY

CALENDAR

Year :
Month :

NOTES

SUNDAY	MONDAY	TUESDAY

"Goodness is the only investment
that never fails." - Henry David Thoreau

WEDNESDAY	THURSDAY	FRIDAY	SATURDAY

CALENDAR

Year :
Month :

NOTES

SUNDAY	MONDAY	TUESDAY

"If you want your children to turn out well, invest twice as much time with them and half as much money." - Abigail Van Buren

WEDNESDAY	THURSDAY	FRIDAY	SATURDAY

MARKET SENTIMENTS / PROSPECTS

DATE

DATE

DATE

DATE

DATE

"Opportunities multiply as they are seized."
- Sun Tzu

CHARTING

FEAR & GREED INDEX

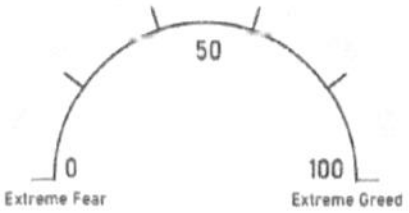

0 Extreme Fear
25 Fear
50 Neutral
75 Greed
100 Extreme Greed

Snapshot of :

Date :

PRICE

TIME

FEAR & GREED INDEX

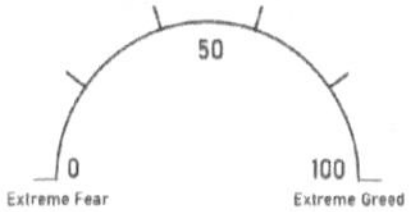

0 Extreme Fear
25 Fear
50 Neutral
75 Greed
100 Extreme Greed

Snapshot of :

Date :

PRICE

TIME

FEAR & GREED INDEX

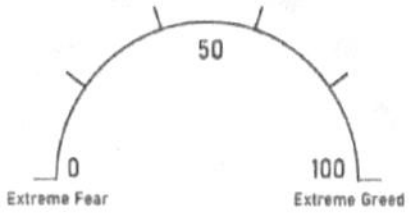

0 Extreme Fear
25 Fear
50 Neutral
75 Greed
100 Extreme Greed

Snapshot of :

Date :

PRICE

TIME

FEAR & GREED INDEX

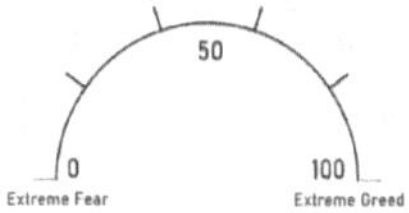

0 Extreme Fear
25 Fear
50 Neutral
75 Greed
100 Extreme Greed

Snapshot of :

Date :

PRICE

TIME

FEAR & GREED INDEX

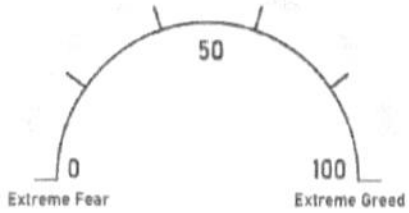

0 Extreme Fear
25 Fear
50 Neutral
75 Greed
100 Extreme Greed

Snapshot of :

Date :

PRICE

TIME

MARKET SENTIMENTS / PROSPECTS

DATE

DATE

DATE

DATE

DATE

"If everyone is thinking alike, then somebody isn't thinking." - General Patton

CHARTING

FEAR & GREED INDEX

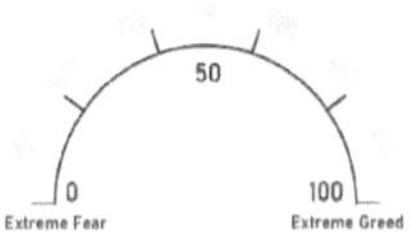

0 Extreme Fear
25 Fear
50 Neutral
75 Greed
100 Extreme Greed

Snapshot of :

Date :

FEAR & GREED INDEX

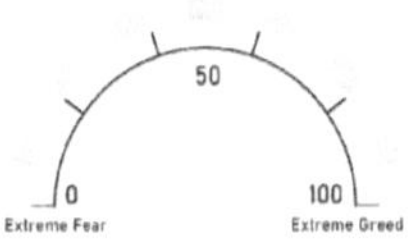

0 Extreme Fear
25 Fear
50 Neutral
75 Greed
100 Extreme Greed

Snapshot of :

Date :

FEAR & GREED INDEX

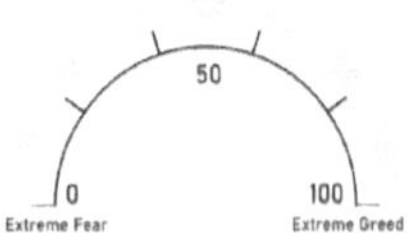

0 Extreme Fear
25 Fear
50 Neutral
75 Greed
100 Extreme Greed

Snapshot of :

Date :

FEAR & GREED INDEX

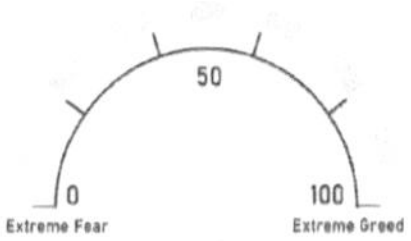

0 Extreme Fear
25 Fear
50 Neutral
75 Greed
100 Extreme Greed

Snapshot of :

Date :

FEAR & GREED INDEX

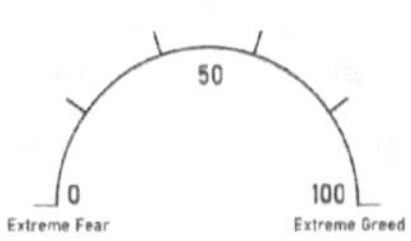

0 Extreme Fear
25 Fear
50 Neutral
75 Greed
100 Extreme Greed

Snapshot of :

Date :

MARKET SENTIMENTS / PROSPECTS

DATE

DATE

DATE

DATE

DATE

"You never know what worse luck your bad luck has saved you from." - Cormac McCarthy

CHARTING

FEAR & GREED INDEX

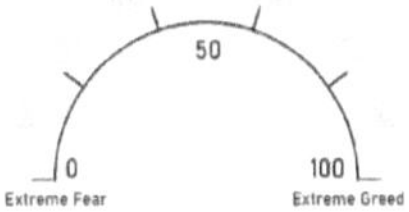

0 Extreme Fear
25 Fear
50 Neutral
75 Greed
100 Extreme Greed

Snapshot of :

Date :

PRICE

TIME

FEAR & GREED INDEX

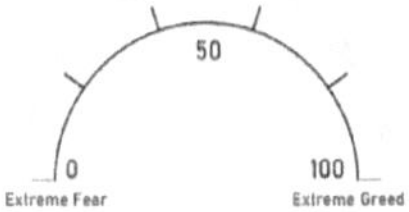

0 Extreme Fear
25 Fear
50 Neutral
75 Greed
100 Extreme Greed

Snapshot of :

Date :

PRICE

TIME

FEAR & GREED INDEX

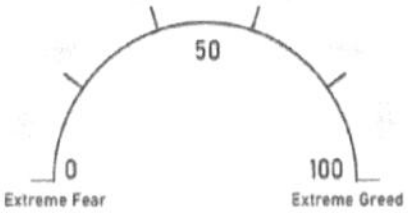

0 Extreme Fear
25 Fear
50 Neutral
75 Greed
100 Extreme Greed

Snapshot of :

Date :

PRICE

TIME

FEAR & GREED INDEX

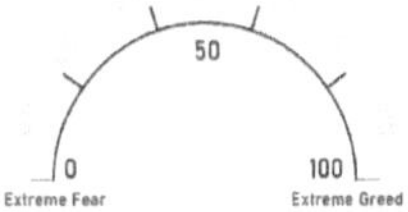

0 Extreme Fear
25 Fear
50 Neutral
75 Greed
100 Extreme Greed

Snapshot of :

Date :

PRICE

TIME

FEAR & GREED INDEX

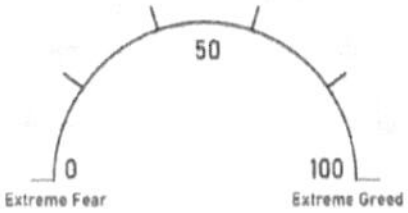

0 Extreme Fear
25 Fear
50 Neutral
75 Greed
100 Extreme Greed

Snapshot of :

Date :

PRICE

TIME

MARKET SENTIMENTS / PROSPECTS

DATE

DATE

DATE

DATE

DATE

"The biggest risk of all is not taking one."
- Mellody Hobson

CHARTING

FEAR & GREED INDEX

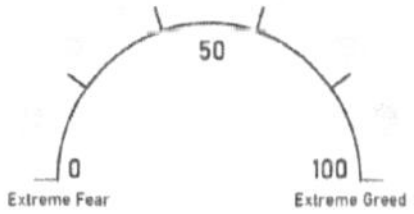

0 Extreme Fear
25 Fear
50 Neutral
75 Greed
100 Extreme Greed

Snapshot of :

Date :

PRICE

TIME

FEAR & GREED INDEX

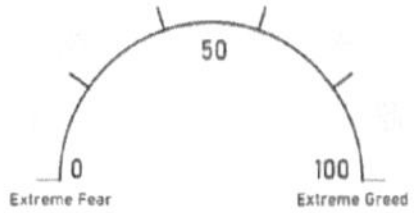

0 Extreme Fear
25 Fear
50 Neutral
75 Greed
100 Extreme Greed

Snapshot of :

Date :

PRICE

TIME

FEAR & GREED INDEX

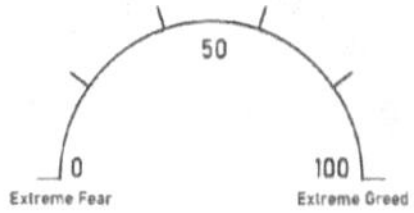

0 Extreme Fear
25 Fear
50 Neutral
75 Greed
100 Extreme Greed

Snapshot of :

Date :

PRICE

TIME

FEAR & GREED INDEX

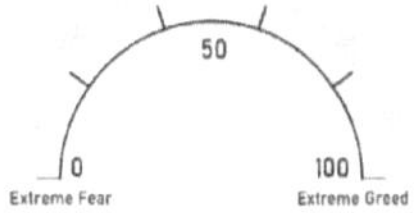

0 Extreme Fear
25 Fear
50 Neutral
75 Greed
100 Extreme Greed

Snapshot of :

Date :

PRICE

TIME

FEAR & GREED INDEX

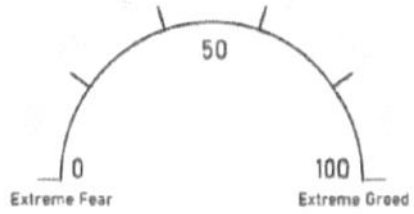

0 Extreme Fear
25 Fear
50 Neutral
75 Greed
100 Extreme Greed

Snapshot of :

Date :

PRICE

TIME

MARKET SENTIMENTS / PROSPECTS

DATE

DATE

DATE

DATE

DATE

"Behind every stock is a company. Find out what it's doing." - Peter Lynch

CHARTING

FEAR & GREED INDEX

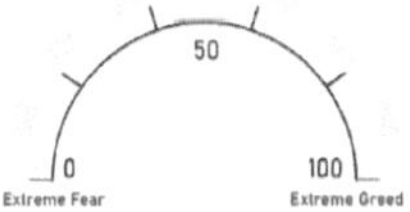

0 Extreme Fear
25 Fear
50 Neutral
75 Greed
100 Extreme Greed

Snapshot of :

Date :

PRICE

TIME

FEAR & GREED INDEX

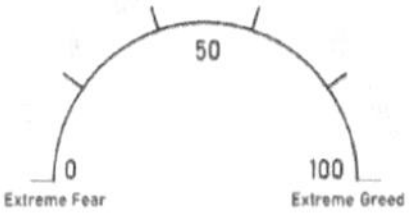

0 Extreme Fear
25 Fear
50 Neutral
75 Greed
100 Extreme Greed

Snapshot of :

Date :

PRICE

TIME

FEAR & GREED INDEX

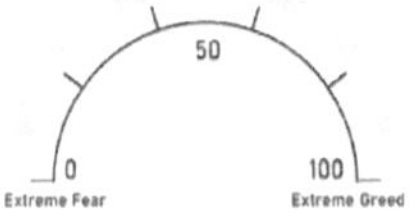

0 Extreme Fear
25 Fear
50 Neutral
75 Greed
100 Extreme Greed

Snapshot of :

Date :

PRICE

TIME

FEAR & GREED INDEX

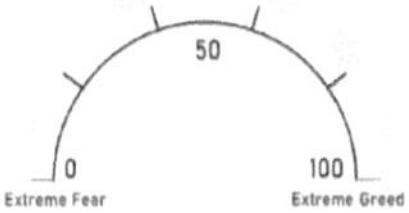

0 Extreme Fear
25 Fear
50 Neutral
75 Greed
100 Extreme Greed

Snapshot of :

Date :

PRICE

TIME

FEAR & GREED INDEX

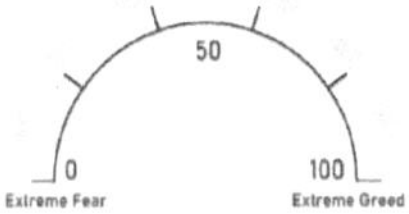

0 Extreme Fear
25 Fear
50 Neutral
75 Greed
100 Extreme Greed

Snapshot of :

Date :

PRICE

TIME

MARKET SENTIMENTS / PROSPECTS

DATE

DATE

DATE

DATE

DATE

"An investment in knowledge pays the best interest." - Benjamin Franklin

CHARTING

FEAR & GREED INDEX

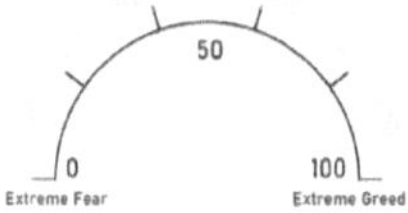

0 Extreme Fear
25 Fear
50 Neutral
75 Greed
100 Extreme Greed

Snapshot of :

Date :

PRICE

TIME

FEAR & GREED INDEX

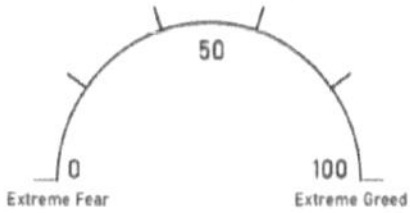

0 Extreme Fear
25 Fear
50 Neutral
75 Greed
100 Extreme Greed

Snapshot of :

Date :

PRICE

TIME

FEAR & GREED INDEX

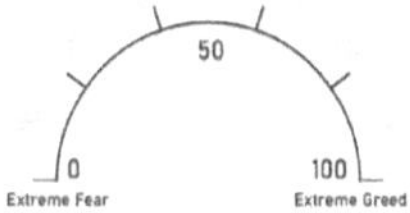

0 Extreme Fear
25 Fear
50 Neutral
75 Greed
100 Extreme Greed

Snapshot of :

Date :

PRICE

TIME

FEAR & GREED INDEX

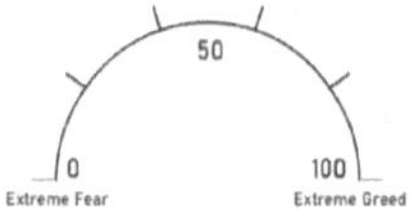

0 Extreme Fear
25 Fear
50 Neutral
75 Greed
100 Extreme Greed

Snapshot of :

Date :

PRICE

TIME

FEAR & GREED INDEX

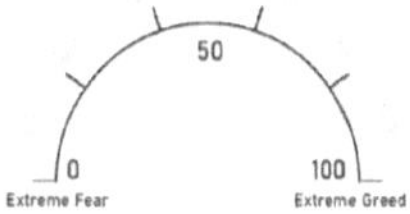

0 Extreme Fear
25 Fear
50 Neutral
75 Greed
100 Extreme Greed

Snapshot of :

Date :

PRICE

TIME

TRADING JOURNAL

Buy/ Sell	Descrption of property: Name (ticker ID)	Descrption of property: QTY (# of shares/tokens)	Date (time) acquired	Date (time) sold/ disposed	Proceeds (sales price)

Cost or other basis (fee included)	Cost per unit	Gain or loss	Fee Reference	Comments (conversion, order #)

TRADING JOURNAL

Buy/ Sell	Descrption of property: Name (ticker ID)	Descrption of property: QTY (# of shares/tokens)	Date (time) acquired	Date (time) sold/ disposed	Proceeds (sales price)

Cost or other basis (fee included)	Cost per unit	Gain or loss	Fee Reference	Comments (conversion, order #)

TRADING JOURNAL

Buy/ Sell	Descrption of property: Name (ticker ID)	Descrption of property: QTY (# of shares/tokens)	Date (time) acquired	Date (time) sold/ disposed	Proceeds (sales price)

Cost or other basis (fee included)	Cost per unit	Gain or loss	Fee Reference	Comments (conversion, order #)

TRADING JOURNAL

Buy/ Sell	Descrption of property: Name (ticker ID)	Descrption of property: QTY (# of shares/tokens)	Date (time) acquired	Date (time) sold/ disposed	Proceeds (sales price)

Cost or other basis (fee included)	Cost per unit	Gain or loss	Fee Reference	Comments (conversion, order #)

TRADING JOURNAL

Buy/ Sell	Descrption of property: Name (ticker ID)	Descrption of property: QTY (# of shares/tokens)	Date (time) acquired	Date (time) sold/ disposed	Proceeds (sales price)

Cost or other basis (fee included)	Cost per unit	Gain or loss	Fee Reference	Comments (conversion, order #)

TRADING JOURNAL

Buy/ Sell	Descrption of property: Name (ticker ID)	Descrption of property: QTY (# of shares/tokens)	Date (time) acquired	Date (time) sold/ disposed	Proceeds (sales price)

Cost or other basis (fee included)	Cost per unit	Gain or loss	Fee Reference	Comments (conversion, order #)

TRADING JOURNAL

Buy/ Sell	Descrption of property: Name (ticker ID)	Descrption of property: QTY (# of shares/tokens)	Date (time) acquired	Date (time) sold/ disposed	Proceeds (sales price)

Cost or other basis (fee included)	Cost per unit	Gain or loss	Fee Reference	Comments (conversion, order #)

TRADING JOURNAL

Buy/ Sell	Descrption of property: Name (ticker ID)	Descrption of property: QTY (# of shares/tokens)	Date (time) acquired	Date (time) sold/ disposed	Proceeds (sales price)

Cost or other basis (fee included)	Cost per unit	Gain or loss	Fee Reference	Comments (conversion, order #)

TRADING JOURNAL

Buy/ Sell	Descrption of property: Name (ticker ID)	Descrption of property: QTY (# of shares/tokens)	Date (time) acquired	Date (time) sold/ disposed	Proceeds (sales price)

Cost or other basis (fee included)	Cost per unit	Gain or loss	Fee Reference	Comments (conversion, order #)

TRADING JOURNAL

Buy/ Sell	Descrption of property: Name (ticker ID)	Descrption of property: QTY (# of shares/tokens)	Date (time) acquired	Date (time) sold/ disposed	Proceeds (sales price)

Cost or other basis (fee included)	Cost per unit	Gain or loss	Fee Reference	Comments (conversion, order #)

TRADING JOURNAL

Buy/ Sell	Descrption of property: Name (ticker ID)	Descrption of property: QTY (# of shares/tokens)	Date (time) acquired	Date (time) sold/ disposed	Proceeds (sales price)

Cost or other basis (fee included)	Cost per unit	Gain or loss	Fee Reference	Comments (conversion, order #)

TRADING JOURNAL

Buy/ Sell	Descrption of property: Name (ticker ID)	Descrption of property: QTY (# of shares/tokens)	Date (time) acquired	Date (time) sold/ disposed	Proceeds (sales price)

Cost or other basis (fee included)	Cost per unit	Gain or loss	Fee Reference	Comments (conversion, order #)

TRADING JOURNAL

Buy/ Sell	Descrption of property: Name (ticker ID)	Descrption of property: QTY (# of shares/tokens)	Date (time) acquired	Date (time) sold/ disposed	Proceeds (sales price)

Cost or other basis (fee included)	Cost per unit	Gain or loss	Fee Reference	Comments (conversion, order #)

TRADING JOURNAL

Buy/ Sell	Descrption of property: Name (ticker ID)	Descrption of property: QTY (# of shares/tokens)	Date (time) acquired	Date (time) sold/ disposed	Proceeds (sales price)

Cost or other basis (fee included)	Cost per unit	Gain or loss	Fee Reference	Comments (conversion, order #)

TRADING JOURNAL

Buy/ Sell	Descrption of property: Name (ticker ID)	Descrption of property: QTY (# of shares/tokens)	Date (time) acquired	Date (time) sold/ disposed	Proceeds (sales price)

Cost or other basis (fee included)	Cost per unit	Gain or loss	Fee Reference	Comments (conversion, order #)

TRADING JOURNAL

Buy/ Sell	Descrption of property: Name (ticker ID)	Descrption of property: QTY (# of shares/tokens)	Date (time) acquired	Date (time) sold/ disposed	Proceeds (sales price)

Cost or other basis (fee included)	Cost per unit	Gain or loss	Fee Reference	Comments (conversion, order #)

TRADING JOURNAL

Buy/ Sell	Descrption of property: Name (ticker ID)	Descrption of property: QTY (# of shares/tokens)	Date (time) acquired	Date (time) sold/ disposed	Proceeds (sales price)

Cost or other basis (fee included)	Cost per unit	Gain or loss	Fee Reference	Comments (conversion, order #)

A I U A

Buy/ Sell	Descrption of property: Name (ticker ID)	Descrption of property: QTY (# of shares/tokens)	Date (time) acquired	Date (time) sold/ disposed	Proceeds (sales price)

Cost or other basis (fee included)	Cost per unit	Gain or loss	Fee Reference	Comments (conversion, order #)

TRADING JOURNAL

Buy/ Sell	Descrption of property: Name (ticker ID)	Descrption of property: QTY (# of shares/tokens)	Date (time) acquired	Date (time) sold/ disposed	Proceeds (sales price)

Cost or other basis (fee included)	Cost per unit	Gain or loss	Fee Reference	Comments (conversion, order #)

TRADING JOURNAL

Buy/ Sell	Descrption of property: Name (ticker ID)	Descrption of property: QTY (# of shares/tokens)	Date (time) acquired	Date (time) sold/ disposed	Proceeds (sales price)

Cost or other basis (fee included)	Cost per unit	Gain or loss	Fee Reference	Comments (conversion, order #)

TRADING JOURNAL

Buy/ Sell	Descrption of property: Name (ticker ID)	Descrption of property: QTY (# of shares/tokens)	Date (time) acquired	Date (time) sold/ disposed	Proceeds (sales price)

Cost or other basis (fee included)	Cost per unit	Gain or loss	Fee Reference	Comments (conversion, order #)

TRADING JOURNAL

Buy/ Sell	Descrption of property: Name (ticker ID)	Descrption of property: QTY (# of shares/tokens)	Date (time) acquired	Date (time) sold/ disposed	Proceeds (sales price)

Cost or other basis (fee included)	Cost per unit	Gain or loss	Fee Reference	Comments (conversion, order #)

TRADING JOURNAL

Buy/ Sell	Descrption of property: Name (ticker ID)	Descrption of property: QTY (# of shares/tokens)	Date (time) acquired	Date (time) sold/ disposed	Proceeds (sales price)

Cost or other basis (fee included)	Cost per unit	Gain or loss	Fee Reference	Comments (conversion, order #)

TRADING JOURNAL

Buy/ Sell	Descrption of property: Name (ticker ID)	Descrption of property: QTY (# of shares/tokens)	Date (time) acquired	Date (time) sold/ disposed	Proceeds (sales price)

Cost or other basis (fee included)	Cost per unit	Gain or loss	Fee Reference	Comments (conversion, order #)

TRADING JOURNAL

Buy/ Sell	Descrption of property: Name (ticker ID)	Descrption of property: QTY (# of shares/tokens)	Date (time) acquired	Date (time) sold/ disposed	Proceeds (sales price)

Cost or other basis (fee included)	Cost per unit	Gain or loss	Fee Reference	Comments (conversion, order #)

TRADING JOURNAL

Buy/ Sell	Descrption of property: Name (ticker ID)	Descrption of property: QTY (# of shares/tokens)	Date (time) acquired	Date (time) sold/ disposed	Proceeds (sales price)

Cost or other basis (fee included)	Cost per unit	Gain or loss	Fee Reference	Comments (conversion, order #)

TRADING JOURNAL

Buy/ Sell	Descrption of property: Name (ticker ID)	Descrption of property: QTY (# of shares/tokens)	Date (time) acquired	Date (time) sold/ disposed	Proceeds (sales price)

Cost or other basis (fee included)	Cost per unit	Gain or loss	Fee Reference	Comments (conversion, order #)

TRADING JOURNAL

Buy/ Sell	Descrption of property: Name (ticker ID)	Descrption of property: QTY (# of shares/tokens)	Date (time) acquired	Date (time) sold/ disposed	Proceeds (sales price)

Cost or other basis (fee included)	Cost per unit	Gain or loss	Fee Reference	Comments (conversion, order #)

TRADING JOURNAL

Buy/ Sell	Descrption of property: Name (ticker ID)	Descrption of property: QTY (# of shares/tokens)	Date (time) acquired	Date (time) sold/ disposed	Proceeds (sales price)

Cost or other basis (fee included)	Cost per unit	Gain or loss	Fee Reference	Comments (conversion, order #)

TRADING JOURNAL

Buy/ Sell	Descrption of property: Name (ticker ID)	Descrption of property: QTY (# of shares/tokens)	Date (time) acquired	Date (time) sold/ disposed	Proceeds (sales price)

Cost or other basis (fee included)	Cost per unit	Gain or loss	Fee Reference	Comments (conversion, order #)

TRADING JOURNAL

Buy/ Sell	Descrption of property: Name (ticker ID)	Descrption of property: QTY (# of shares/tokens)	Date (time) acquired	Date (time) sold/ disposed	Proceeds (sales price)

Cost or other basis (fee included)	Cost per unit	Gain or loss	Fee Reference	Comments (conversion, order #)

TRADING JOURNAL

Buy/ Sell	Descrption of property: Name (ticker ID)	Descrption of property: QTY (# of shares/tokens)	Date (time) acquired	Date (time) sold/ disposed	Proceeds (sales price)

Cost or other basis (fee included)	Cost per unit	Gain or loss	Fee Reference	Comments (conversion, order #)

TRADING JOURNAL

Buy/ Sell	Descrption of property: Name (ticker ID)	Descrption of property: QTY (# of shares/tokens)	Date (time) acquired	Date (time) sold/ disposed	Proceeds (sales price)

Cost or other basis (fee included)	Cost per unit	Gain or loss	Fee Reference	Comments (conversion, order #)

TRADING JOURNAL

Buy/ Sell	Descrption of property: Name (ticker ID)	Descrption of property: QTY (# of shares/tokens)	Date (time) acquired	Date (time) sold/ disposed	Proceeds (sales price)

Cost or other basis (fee included)	Cost per unit	Gain or loss	Fee Reference	Comments (conversion, order #)

TRADING JOURNAL

Buy/ Sell	Descrption of property: Name (ticker ID)	Descrption of property: QTY (# of shares/tokens)	Date (time) acquired	Date (time) sold/ disposed	Proceeds (sales price)

Cost or other basis (fee included)	Cost per unit	Gain or loss	Fee Reference	Comments (conversion, order #)

TRADING JOURNAL

Buy/ Sell	Descrption of property: Name (ticker ID)	Descrption of property: QTY (# of shares/tokens)	Date (time) acquired	Date (time) sold/ disposed	Proceeds (sales price)

Cost or other basis (fee included)	Cost per unit	Gain or loss	Fee Reference	Comments (conversion, order #)

TRADING JOURNAL

Buy/ Sell	Descrption of property: Name (ticker ID)	Descrption of property: QTY (# of shares/tokens)	Date (time) acquired	Date (time) sold/ disposed	Proceeds (sales price)

Cost or other basis (fee included)	Cost per unit	Gain or loss	Fee Reference	Comments (conversion, order #)

TRADING JOURNAL

Buy/ Sell	Descrption of property: Name (ticker ID)	Descrption of property: QTY (# of shares/tokens)	Date (time) acquired	Date (time) sold/ disposed	Proceeds (sales price)

Cost or other basis (fee included)	Cost per unit	Gain or loss	Fee Reference	Comments (conversion, order #)

TRADING JOURNAL

Buy/ Sell	Descrption of property: Name (ticker ID)	Descrption of property: QTY (# of shares/tokens)	Date (time) acquired	Date (time) sold/ disposed	Proceeds (sales price)

Cost or other basis (fee included)	Cost per unit	Gain or loss	Fee Reference	Comments (conversion, order #)

TRADING JOURNAL

Buy/ Sell	Descrption of property: Name (ticker ID)	Descrption of property: QTY (# of shares/tokens)	Date (time) acquired	Date (time) sold/ disposed	Proceeds (sales price)

Cost or other basis (fee included)	Cost per unit	Gain or loss	Fee Reference	Comments (conversion, order #)

TRADING JOURNAL

Buy/ Sell	Descrption of property: Name (ticker ID)	Descrption of property: QTY (# of shares/tokens)	Date (time) acquired	Date (time) sold/ disposed	Proceeds (sales price)

Cost or other basis (fee included)	Cost per unit	Gain or loss	Fee Reference	Comments (conversion, order #)

TRADING JOURNAL

Buy/ Sell	Descrption of property: Name (ticker ID)	Descrption of property: QTY (# of shares/tokens)	Date (time) acquired	Date (time) sold/ disposed	Proceeds (sales price)

Cost or other basis (fee included)	Cost per unit	Gain or loss	Fee Reference	Comments (conversion, order #)

TRADING JOURNAL

Buy/ Sell	Descrption of property: Name (ticker ID)	Descrption of property: QTY (# of shares/tokens)	Date (time) acquired	Date (time) sold/ disposed	Proceeds (sales price)

Cost or other basis (fee included)	Cost per unit	Gain or loss	Fee Reference	Comments (conversion, order #)

TRADING JOURNAL

Buy/ Sell	Descrption of property: Name (ticker ID)	Descrption of property: QTY (# of shares/tokens)	Date (time) acquired	Date (time) sold/ disposed	Proceeds (sales price)

Cost or other basis (fee included)	Cost per unit	Gain or loss	Fee Reference	Comments (conversion, order #)

TRADING JOURNAL

Buy/ Sell	Descrption of property: Name (ticker ID)	Descrption of property: QTY (# of shares/tokens)	Date (time) acquired	Date (time) sold/ disposed	Proceeds (sales price)

Cost or other basis (fee included)	Cost per unit	Gain or loss	Fee Reference	Comments (conversion, order #)

TRADING JOURNAL

Buy/ Sell	Descrption of property: Name (ticker ID)	Descrption of property: QTY (# of shares/tokens)	Date (time) acquired	Date (time) sold/ disposed	Proceeds (sales price)

Cost or other basis (fee included)	Cost per unit	Gain or loss	Fee Reference	Comments (conversion, order #)

TRADING JOURNAL

Buy/ Sell	Descrption of property: Name (ticker ID)	Descrption of property: QTY (# of shares/tokens)	Date (time) acquired	Date (time) sold/ disposed	Proceeds (sales price)

Cost or other basis (fee included)	Cost per unit	Gain or loss	Fee Reference	Comments (conversion, order #)

TRADING JOURNAL

Buy/ Sell	Descrption of property: Name (ticker ID)	Descrption of property: QTY (# of shares/tokens)	Date (time) acquired	Date (time) sold/ disposed	Proceeds (sales price)

Cost or other basis (fee included)	Cost per unit	Gain or loss	Fee Reference	Comments (conversion, order #)

TRADING JOURNAL

Buy/ Sell	Descrption of property: Name (ticker ID)	Descrption of property: QTY (# of shares/tokens)	Date (time) acquired	Date (time) sold/ disposed	Proceeds (sales price)

Cost or other basis (fee included)	Cost per unit	Gain or loss	Fee Reference	Comments (conversion, order #)

TRADING JOURNAL

Buy/ Sell	Descrption of property: Name (ticker ID)	Descrption of property: QTY (# of shares/tokens)	Date (time) acquired	Date (time) sold/ disposed	Proceeds (sales price)

Cost or other basis (fee included)	Cost per unit	Gain or loss	Fee Reference	Comments (conversion, order #)

TRADING JOURNAL

Buy/ Sell	Descrption of property: Name (ticker ID)	Descrption of property: QTY (# of shares/tokens)	Date (time) acquired	Date (time) sold/ disposed	Proceeds (sales price)

Cost or other basis (fee included)	Cost per unit	Gain or loss	Fee Reference	Comments (conversion, order #)

BIP39 Wordlist

#	word	#	word	#	word	#	word
1	abandon	513	divorce	1025	length	1537	scale
2	ability	514	dizzy	1026	lens	1538	scan
3	able	515	doctor	1027	leopard	1539	scare
4	about	516	document	1028	lesson	1540	scatter
5	above	517	dog	1029	letter	1541	scene
6	absent	518	doll	1030	level	1542	scheme
7	absorb	519	dolphin	1031	liar	1543	school
8	abstract	520	domain	1032	liberty	1544	science
9	absurd	521	donate	1033	library	1545	scissors
10	abuse	522	donkey	1034	license	1546	scorpion
11	access	523	donor	1035	life	1547	scout
12	accident	524	door	1036	lift	1548	scrap
13	account	525	dose	1037	light	1549	screen
14	accuse	526	double	1038	like	1550	script
15	achieve	527	dove	1039	limb	1551	scrub
16	acid	528	draft	1040	limit	1552	sea
17	acoustic	529	dragon	1041	link	1553	search
18	acquire	530	drama	1042	lion	1554	season
19	across	531	drastic	1043	liquid	1555	seat
20	act	532	draw	1044	list	1556	second
21	action	533	dream	1045	little	1557	secret
22	actor	534	dress	1046	live	1558	section
23	actress	535	drift	1047	lizard	1559	security
24	actual	536	drill	1048	load	1560	seed
25	adapt	537	drink	1049	loan	1561	seek
26	add	538	drip	1050	lobster	1562	segment
27	addict	539	drive	1051	local	1563	select
28	address	540	drop	1052	lock	1564	sell
29	adjust	541	drum	1053	logic	1565	seminar
30	admit	542	dry	1054	lonely	1566	senior
31	adult	543	duck	1055	long	1567	sense
32	advance	544	dumb	1056	loop	1568	sentence
33	advice	545	dune	1057	lottery	1569	series
34	aerobic	546	during	1058	loud	1570	service
35	affair	547	dust	1059	lounge	1571	session
36	afford	548	dutch	1060	love	1572	settle
37	afraid	549	duty	1061	loyal	1573	setup
38	again	550	dwarf	1062	lucky	1574	seven
39	age	551	dynamic	1063	luggage	1575	shadow
40	agent	552	eager	1064	lumber	1576	shaft
41	agree	553	eagle	1065	lunar	1577	shallow
42	ahead	554	early	1066	lunch	1578	share
43	aim	555	earn	1067	luxury	1579	shed
44	air	556	earth	1068	lyrics	1580	shell
45	airport	557	easily	1069	machine	1581	sheriff
46	aisle	558	east	1070	mad	1582	shield
47	alarm	559	easy	1071	magic	1583	shift
48	album	560	echo	1072	magnet	1584	shine
49	alcohol	561	ecology	1073	maid	1585	ship
50	alert	562	economy	1074	mail	1586	shiver
51	alien	563	edge	1075	main	1587	shock
52	all	564	edit	1076	major	1588	shoe
53	alley	565	educate	1077	make	1589	shoot
54	allow	566	effort	1078	mammal	1590	shop
55	almost	567	egg	1079	man	1591	short
56	alone	568	eight	1080	manage	1592	shoulder
57	alpha	569	either	1081	mandate	1593	shove
58	already	570	elbow	1082	mango	1594	shrimp
59	also	571	elder	1083	mansion	1595	shrug
60	alter	572	electric	1084	manual	1596	shuffle
61	always	573	elegant	1085	maple	1597	shy
62	amateur	574	element	1086	marble	1598	sibling
63	amazing	575	elephant	1087	march	1599	sick
64	among	576	elevator	1088	margin	1600	side

#	word	#	word	#	word	#	word
65	amount	577	elite	1089	marine	1601	siege
66	amused	578	else	1090	market	1602	sight
67	analyst	579	embark	1091	marriage	1603	sign
68	anchor	580	embody	1092	mask	1604	silent
69	ancient	581	embrace	1093	mass	1605	silk
70	anger	582	emerge	1094	master	1606	silly
71	angle	583	emotion	1095	match	1607	silver
72	angry	584	employ	1096	material	1608	similar
73	animal	585	empower	1097	math	1609	simple
74	ankle	586	empty	1098	matrix	1610	since
75	announce	587	enable	1099	matter	1611	sing
76	annual	588	enact	1100	maximum	1612	siren
77	another	589	end	1101	maze	1613	sister
78	answer	590	endless	1102	meadow	1614	situate
79	antenna	591	endorse	1103	mean	1615	six
80	antique	592	enemy	1104	measure	1616	size
81	anxiety	593	energy	1105	meat	1617	skate
82	any	594	enforce	1106	mechanic	1618	sketch
83	apart	595	engage	1107	medal	1619	ski
84	apology	596	engine	1108	media	1620	skill
85	appear	597	enhance	1109	melody	1621	skin
86	apple	598	enjoy	1110	melt	1622	skirt
87	approve	599	enlist	1111	member	1623	skull
88	april	600	enough	1112	memory	1624	slab
89	arch	601	enrich	1113	mention	1625	slam
90	arctic	602	enroll	1114	menu	1626	sleep
91	area	603	ensure	1115	mercy	1627	slender
92	arena	604	enter	1116	merge	1628	slice
93	argue	605	entire	1117	merit	1629	slide
94	arm	606	entry	1118	merry	1630	slight
95	armed	607	envelope	1119	mesh	1631	slim
96	armor	608	episode	1120	message	1632	slogan
97	army	609	equal	1121	metal	1633	slot
98	around	610	equip	1122	method	1634	slow
99	arrange	611	era	1123	middle	1635	slush
100	arrest	612	erase	1124	midnight	1636	small
101	arrive	613	erode	1125	milk	1637	smart
102	arrow	614	erosion	1126	million	1638	smile
103	art	615	error	1127	mimic	1639	smoke
104	artefact	616	erupt	1128	mind	1640	smooth
105	artist	617	escape	1129	minimum	1641	snack
106	artwork	618	essay	1130	minor	1642	snake
107	ask	619	essence	1131	minute	1643	snap
108	aspect	620	estate	1132	miracle	1644	sniff
109	assault	621	eternal	1133	mirror	1645	snow
110	asset	622	ethics	1134	misery	1646	soap
111	assist	623	evidence	1135	miss	1647	soccer
112	assume	624	evil	1136	mistake	1648	social
113	asthma	625	evoke	1137	mix	1649	sock
114	athlete	626	evolve	1138	mixed	1650	soda
115	atom	627	exact	1139	mixture	1651	soft
116	attack	628	example	1140	mobile	1652	solar
117	attend	629	excess	1141	model	1653	soldier
118	attitude	630	exchange	1142	modify	1654	solid
119	attract	631	excite	1143	mom	1655	solution
120	auction	632	exclude	1144	moment	1656	solve
121	audit	633	excuse	1145	monitor	1657	someone
122	august	634	execute	1146	monkey	1658	song
123	aunt	635	exercise	1147	monster	1659	soon
124	author	636	exhaust	1148	month	1660	sorry
125	auto	637	exhibit	1149	moon	1661	sort
126	autumn	638	exile	1150	moral	1662	soul
127	average	639	exist	1151	more	1663	sound
128	avocado	640	exit	1152	morning	1664	soup
129	avoid	641	exotic	1153	mosquito	1665	source

#	word	#	word	#	word	#	word
130	awake	642	expand	1154	mother	1666	south
131	aware	643	expect	1155	motion	1667	space
132	away	644	expire	1156	motor	1668	spare
133	awesome	645	explain	1157	mountain	1669	spatial
134	awful	646	expose	1158	mouse	1670	spawn
135	awkward	647	express	1159	move	1671	speak
136	axis	648	extend	1160	movie	1672	special
137	baby	649	extra	1161	much	1673	speed
138	bachelor	650	eye	1162	muffin	1674	spell
139	bacon	651	eyebrow	1163	mule	1675	spend
140	badge	652	fabric	1164	multiply	1676	sphere
141	bag	653	face	1165	muscle	1677	spice
142	balance	654	faculty	1166	museum	1678	spider
143	balcony	655	fade	1167	mushroom	1679	spike
144	ball	656	faint	1168	music	1680	spin
145	bamboo	657	faith	1169	must	1681	spirit
146	banana	658	fall	1170	mutual	1682	split
147	banner	659	false	1171	myself	1683	spoil
148	bar	660	fame	1172	mystery	1684	sponsor
149	barely	661	family	1173	myth	1685	spoon
150	bargain	662	famous	1174	naive	1686	sport
151	barrel	663	fan	1175	name	1687	spot
152	base	664	fancy	1176	napkin	1688	spray
153	basic	665	fantasy	1177	narrow	1689	spread
154	basket	666	farm	1178	nasty	1690	spring
155	battle	667	fashion	1179	nation	1691	spy
156	beach	668	fat	1180	nature	1692	square
157	bean	669	fatal	1181	near	1693	squeeze
158	beauty	670	father	1182	neck	1694	squirrel
159	because	671	fatigue	1183	need	1695	stable
160	become	672	fault	1184	negative	1696	stadium
161	beef	673	favorite	1185	neglect	1697	staff
162	before	674	feature	1186	neither	1698	stage
163	begin	675	february	1187	nephew	1699	stairs
164	behave	676	federal	1188	nerve	1700	stamp
165	behind	677	fee	1189	nest	1701	stand
166	believe	678	feed	1190	net	1702	start
167	below	679	feel	1191	network	1703	state
168	belt	680	female	1192	neutral	1704	stay
169	bench	681	fence	1193	never	1705	steak
170	benefit	682	festival	1194	news	1706	steel
171	best	683	fetch	1195	next	1707	stem
172	betray	684	fever	1196	nice	1708	step
173	better	685	few	1197	night	1709	stereo
174	between	686	fiber	1198	noble	1710	stick
175	beyond	687	fiction	1199	noise	1711	still
176	bicycle	688	field	1200	nominee	1712	sting
177	bid	689	figure	1201	noodle	1713	stock
178	bike	690	file	1202	normal	1714	stomach
179	bind	691	film	1203	north	1715	stone
180	biology	692	filter	1204	nose	1716	stool
181	bird	693	final	1205	notable	1717	story
182	birth	694	find	1206	note	1718	stove
183	bitter	695	fine	1207	nothing	1719	strategy
184	black	696	finger	1208	notice	1720	street
185	blade	697	finish	1209	novel	1721	strike
186	blame	698	fire	1210	now	1722	strong
187	blanket	699	firm	1211	nuclear	1723	struggle
188	blast	700	first	1212	number	1724	student
189	bleak	701	fiscal	1213	nurse	1725	stuff
190	bless	702	fish	1214	nut	1726	stumble
191	blind	703	fit	1215	oak	1727	style
192	blood	704	fitness	1216	obey	1728	subject
193	blossom	705	fix	1217	object	1729	submit
194	blouse	706	flag	1218	oblige	1730	subway

#	word	#	word	#	word	#	word
195	blue	707	flame	1219	obscure	1731	success
196	blur	708	flash	1220	observe	1732	such
197	blush	709	flat	1221	obtain	1733	sudden
198	board	710	flavor	1222	obvious	1734	suffer
199	boat	711	flee	1223	occur	1735	sugar
200	body	712	flight	1224	ocean	1736	suggest
201	boil	713	flip	1225	october	1737	suit
202	bomb	714	float	1226	odor	1738	summer
203	bone	715	flock	1227	off	1739	sun
204	bonus	716	floor	1228	offer	1740	sunny
205	book	717	flower	1229	office	1741	sunset
206	boost	718	fluid	1230	often	1742	super
207	border	719	flush	1231	oil	1743	supply
208	boring	720	fly	1232	okay	1744	supreme
209	borrow	721	foam	1233	old	1745	sure
210	boss	722	focus	1234	olive	1746	surface
211	bottom	723	fog	1235	olympic	1747	surge
212	bounce	724	foil	1236	omit	1748	surprise
213	box	725	fold	1237	once	1749	surround
214	boy	726	follow	1238	one	1750	survey
215	bracket	727	food	1239	onion	1751	suspect
216	brain	728	foot	1240	online	1752	sustain
217	brand	729	force	1241	only	1753	swallow
218	brass	730	forest	1242	open	1754	swamp
219	brave	731	forget	1243	opera	1755	swap
220	bread	732	fork	1244	opinion	1756	swarm
221	breeze	733	fortune	1245	oppose	1757	swear
222	brick	734	forum	1246	option	1758	sweet
223	bridge	735	forward	1247	orange	1759	swift
224	brief	736	fossil	1248	orbit	1760	swim
225	bright	737	foster	1249	orchard	1761	swing
226	bring	738	found	1250	order	1762	switch
227	brisk	739	fox	1251	ordinary	1763	sword
228	broccoli	740	fragile	1252	organ	1764	symbol
229	broken	741	frame	1253	orient	1765	symptom
230	bronze	742	frequent	1254	original	1766	syrup
231	broom	743	fresh	1255	orphan	1767	system
232	brother	744	friend	1256	ostrich	1768	table
233	brown	745	fringe	1257	other	1769	tackle
234	brush	746	frog	1258	outdoor	1770	tag
235	bubble	747	front	1259	outer	1771	tail
236	buddy	748	frost	1260	output	1772	talent
237	budget	749	frown	1261	outside	1773	talk
238	buffalo	750	frozen	1262	oval	1774	tank
239	build	751	fruit	1263	oven	1775	tape
240	bulb	752	fuel	1264	over	1776	target
241	bulk	753	fun	1265	own	1777	task
242	bullet	754	funny	1266	owner	1778	taste
243	bundle	755	furnace	1267	oxygen	1779	tattoo
244	bunker	756	fury	1268	oyster	1780	taxi
245	burden	757	future	1269	ozone	1781	teach
246	burger	758	gadget	1270	pact	1782	team
247	burst	759	gain	1271	paddle	1783	tell
248	bus	760	galaxy	1272	page	1784	ten
249	business	761	gallery	1273	pair	1785	tenant
250	busy	762	game	1274	palace	1786	tennis
251	butter	763	gap	1275	palm	1787	tent
252	buyer	764	garage	1276	panda	1788	term
253	buzz	765	garbage	1277	panel	1789	test
254	cabbage	766	garden	1278	panic	1790	text
255	cabin	767	garlic	1279	panther	1791	thank
256	cable	768	garment	1280	paper	1792	that
257	cactus	769	gas	1281	parade	1793	theme
258	cage	770	gasp	1282	parent	1794	then
259	cake	771	gate	1283	park	1795	theory

#	word	#	word	#	word	#	word
260	call	772	gather	1284	parrot	1796	there
261	calm	773	gauge	1285	party	1797	they
262	camera	774	gaze	1286	pass	1798	thing
263	camp	775	general	1287	patch	1799	this
264	can	776	genius	1288	path	1800	thought
265	canal	777	genre	1289	patient	1801	three
266	cancel	778	gentle	1290	patrol	1802	thrive
267	candy	779	genuine	1291	pattern	1803	throw
268	cannon	780	gesture	1292	pause	1804	thumb
269	canoe	781	ghost	1293	pave	1805	thunder
270	canvas	782	giant	1294	payment	1806	ticket
271	canyon	783	gift	1295	peace	1807	tide
272	capable	784	giggle	1296	peanut	1808	tiger
273	capital	785	ginger	1297	pear	1809	tilt
274	captain	786	giraffe	1298	peasant	1810	timber
275	car	787	girl	1299	pelican	1811	time
276	carbon	788	give	1300	pen	1812	tiny
277	card	789	glad	1301	penalty	1813	tip
278	cargo	790	glance	1302	pencil	1814	tired
279	carpet	791	glare	1303	people	1815	tissue
280	carry	792	glass	1304	pepper	1816	title
281	cart	793	glide	1305	perfect	1817	toast
282	case	794	glimpse	1306	permit	1818	tobacco
283	cash	795	globe	1307	person	1819	today
284	casino	796	gloom	1308	pet	1820	toddler
285	castle	797	glory	1309	phone	1821	toe
286	casual	798	glove	1310	photo	1822	together
287	cat	799	glow	1311	phrase	1823	toilet
288	catalog	800	glue	1312	physical	1824	token
289	catch	801	goat	1313	piano	1825	tomato
290	category	802	goddess	1314	picnic	1826	tomorrow
291	cattle	803	gold	1315	picture	1827	tone
292	caught	804	good	1316	piece	1828	tongue
293	cause	805	goose	1317	pig	1829	tonight
294	caution	806	gorilla	1318	pigeon	1830	tool
295	cave	807	gospel	1319	pill	1831	tooth
296	ceiling	808	gossip	1320	pilot	1832	top
297	celery	809	govern	1321	pink	1833	topic
298	cement	810	gown	1322	pioneer	1834	topple
299	census	811	grab	1323	pipe	1835	torch
300	century	812	grace	1324	pistol	1836	tornado
301	cereal	813	grain	1325	pitch	1837	tortoise
302	certain	814	grant	1326	pizza	1838	toss
303	chair	815	grape	1327	place	1839	total
304	chalk	816	grass	1328	planet	1840	tourist
305	champion	817	gravity	1329	plastic	1841	toward
306	change	818	great	1330	plate	1842	tower
307	chaos	819	green	1331	play	1843	town
308	chapter	820	grid	1332	please	1844	toy
309	charge	821	grief	1333	pledge	1845	track
310	chase	822	grit	1334	pluck	1846	trade
311	chat	823	grocery	1335	plug	1847	traffic
312	cheap	824	group	1336	plunge	1848	tragic
313	check	825	grow	1337	poem	1849	train
314	cheese	826	grunt	1338	poet	1850	transfer
315	chef	827	guard	1339	point	1851	trap
316	cherry	828	guess	1340	polar	1852	trash
317	chest	829	guide	1341	pole	1853	travel
318	chicken	830	guilt	1342	police	1854	tray
319	chief	831	guitar	1343	pond	1855	treat
320	child	832	gun	1344	pony	1856	tree
321	chimney	833	gym	1345	pool	1857	trend
322	choice	834	habit	1346	popular	1858	trial
323	choose	835	hair	1347	portion	1859	tribe
324	chronic	836	half	1348	position	1860	trick

#	word	#	word	#	word	#	word
325	chuckle	837	hammer	1349	possible	1861	trigger
326	chunk	838	hamster	1350	post	1862	trim
327	churn	839	hand	1351	potato	1863	trip
328	cigar	840	happy	1352	pottery	1864	trophy
329	cinnamon	841	harbor	1353	poverty	1865	trouble
330	circle	842	hard	1354	powder	1866	truck
331	citizen	843	harsh	1355	power	1867	true
332	city	844	harvest	1356	practice	1868	truly
333	civil	845	hat	1357	praise	1869	trumpet
334	claim	846	have	1358	predict	1870	trust
335	clap	847	hawk	1359	prefer	1871	truth
336	clarify	848	hazard	1360	prepare	1872	try
337	claw	849	head	1361	present	1873	tube
338	clay	850	health	1362	pretty	1874	tuition
339	clean	851	heart	1363	prevent	1875	tumble
340	clerk	852	heavy	1364	price	1876	tuna
341	clever	853	hedgehog	1365	pride	1877	tunnel
342	click	854	height	1366	primary	1878	turkey
343	client	855	hello	1367	print	1879	turn
344	cliff	856	helmet	1368	priority	1880	turtle
345	climb	857	help	1369	prison	1881	twelve
346	clinic	858	hen	1370	private	1882	twenty
347	clip	859	hero	1371	prize	1883	twice
348	clock	860	hidden	1372	problem	1884	twin
349	clog	861	high	1373	process	1885	twist
350	close	862	hill	1374	produce	1886	two
351	cloth	863	hint	1375	profit	1887	type
352	cloud	864	hip	1376	program	1888	typical
353	clown	865	hire	1377	project	1889	ugly
354	club	866	history	1378	promote	1890	umbrella
355	clump	867	hobby	1379	proof	1891	unable
356	cluster	868	hockey	1380	property	1892	unaware
357	clutch	869	hold	1381	prosper	1893	uncle
358	coach	870	hole	1382	protect	1894	uncover
359	coast	871	holiday	1383	proud	1895	under
360	coconut	872	hollow	1384	provide	1896	undo
361	code	873	home	1385	public	1897	unfair
362	coffee	874	honey	1386	pudding	1898	unfold
363	coil	875	hood	1387	pull	1899	unhappy
364	coin	876	hope	1388	pulp	1900	uniform
365	collect	877	horn	1389	pulse	1901	unique
366	color	878	horror	1390	pumpkin	1902	unit
367	column	879	horse	1391	punch	1903	universe
368	combine	880	hospital	1392	pupil	1904	unknown
369	come	881	host	1393	puppy	1905	unlock
370	comfort	882	hotel	1394	purchase	1906	until
371	comic	883	hour	1395	purity	1907	unusual
372	common	884	hover	1396	purpose	1908	unveil
373	company	885	hub	1397	purse	1909	update
374	concert	886	huge	1398	push	1910	upgrade
375	conduct	887	human	1399	put	1911	uphold
376	confirm	888	humble	1400	puzzle	1912	upon
377	congress	889	humor	1401	pyramid	1913	upper
378	connect	890	hundred	1402	quality	1914	upset
379	consider	891	hungry	1403	quantum	1915	urban
380	control	892	hunt	1404	quarter	1916	urge
381	convince	893	hurdle	1405	question	1917	usage
382	cook	894	hurry	1406	quick	1918	use
383	cool	895	hurt	1407	quit	1919	used
384	copper	896	husband	1408	quiz	1920	useful
385	copy	897	hybrid	1409	quote	1921	useless
386	coral	898	ice	1410	rabbit	1922	usual
387	core	899	icon	1411	raccoon	1923	utility
388	corn	900	idea	1412	race	1924	vacant
389	correct	901	identify	1413	rack	1925	vacuum

#	word	#	word	#	word	#	word
390	cost	902	idle	1414	radar	1926	vague
391	cotton	903	ignore	1415	radio	1927	valid
392	couch	904	ill	1416	rail	1928	valley
393	country	905	illegal	1417	rain	1929	valve
394	couple	906	illness	1418	raise	1930	van
395	course	907	image	1419	rally	1931	vanish
396	cousin	908	imitate	1420	ramp	1932	vapor
397	cover	909	immense	1421	ranch	1933	various
398	coyote	910	immune	1422	random	1934	vast
399	crack	911	impact	1423	range	1935	vault
400	cradle	912	impose	1424	rapid	1936	vehicle
401	craft	913	improve	1425	rare	1937	velvet
402	cram	914	impulse	1426	rate	1938	vendor
403	crane	915	inch	1427	rather	1939	venture
404	crash	916	include	1428	raven	1940	venue
405	crater	917	income	1429	raw	1941	verb
406	crawl	918	increase	1430	razor	1942	verify
407	crazy	919	index	1431	ready	1943	version
408	cream	920	indicate	1432	real	1944	very
409	credit	921	indoor	1433	reason	1945	vessel
410	creek	922	industry	1434	rebel	1946	veteran
411	crew	923	infant	1435	rebuild	1947	viable
412	cricket	924	inflict	1436	recall	1948	vibrant
413	crime	925	inform	1437	receive	1949	vicious
414	crisp	926	inhale	1438	recipe	1950	victory
415	critic	927	inherit	1439	record	1951	video
416	crop	928	initial	1440	recycle	1952	view
417	cross	929	inject	1441	reduce	1953	village
418	crouch	930	injury	1442	reflect	1954	vintage
419	crowd	931	inmate	1443	reform	1955	violin
420	crucial	932	inner	1444	refuse	1956	virtual
421	cruel	933	innocent	1445	region	1957	virus
422	cruise	934	input	1446	regret	1958	visa
423	crumble	935	inquiry	1447	regular	1959	visit
424	crunch	936	insane	1448	reject	1960	visual
425	crush	937	insect	1449	relax	1961	vital
426	cry	938	inside	1450	release	1962	vivid
427	crystal	939	inspire	1451	relief	1963	vocal
428	cube	940	install	1452	rely	1964	voice
429	culture	941	intact	1453	remain	1965	void
430	cup	942	interest	1454	remember	1966	volcano
431	cupboard	943	into	1455	remind	1967	volume
432	curious	944	invest	1456	remove	1968	vote
433	current	945	invite	1457	render	1969	voyage
434	curtain	946	involve	1458	renew	1970	wage
435	curve	947	iron	1459	rent	1971	wagon
436	cushion	948	island	1460	reopen	1972	wait
437	custom	949	isolate	1461	repair	1973	walk
438	cute	950	issue	1462	repeat	1974	wall
439	cycle	951	item	1463	replace	1975	walnut
440	dad	952	ivory	1464	report	1976	want
441	damage	953	jacket	1465	require	1977	warfare
442	damp	954	jaguar	1466	rescue	1978	warm
443	dance	955	jar	1467	resemble	1979	warrior
444	danger	956	jazz	1468	resist	1980	wash
445	daring	957	jealous	1469	resource	1981	wasp
446	dash	958	jeans	1470	response	1982	waste
447	daughter	959	jelly	1471	result	1983	water
448	dawn	960	jewel	1472	retire	1984	wave
449	day	961	job	1473	retreat	1985	way
450	deal	962	join	1474	return	1986	wealth
451	debate	963	joke	1475	reunion	1987	weapon
452	debris	964	journey	1476	reveal	1988	wear
453	decade	965	joy	1477	review	1989	weasel
454	december	966	judge	1478	reward	1990	weather

#	word	#	word	#	word	#	word
455	decide	967	juice	1479	rhythm	1991	web
456	decline	968	jump	1480	rib	1992	wedding
457	decorate	969	jungle	1481	ribbon	1993	weekend
458	decrease	970	junior	1482	rice	1994	weird
459	deer	971	junk	1483	rich	1995	welcome
460	defense	972	just	1484	ride	1996	west
461	define	973	kangaroo	1485	ridge	1997	wet
462	defy	974	keen	1486	rifle	1998	whale
463	degree	975	keep	1487	right	1999	what
464	delay	976	ketchup	1488	rigid	2000	wheat
465	deliver	977	key	1489	ring	2001	wheel
466	demand	978	kick	1490	riot	2002	when
467	demise	979	kid	1491	ripple	2003	where
468	denial	980	kidney	1492	risk	2004	whip
469	dentist	981	kind	1493	ritual	2005	whisper
470	deny	982	kingdom	1494	rival	2006	wide
471	depart	983	kiss	1495	river	2007	width
472	depend	984	kit	1496	road	2008	wife
473	deposit	985	kitchen	1497	roast	2009	wild
474	depth	986	kite	1498	robot	2010	will
475	deputy	987	kitten	1499	robust	2011	win
476	derive	988	kiwi	1500	rocket	2012	window
477	describe	989	knee	1501	romance	2013	wine
478	desert	990	knife	1502	roof	2014	wing
479	design	991	knock	1503	rookie	2015	wink
480	desk	992	know	1504	room	2016	winner
481	despair	993	lab	1505	rose	2017	winter
482	destroy	994	label	1506	rotate	2018	wire
483	detail	995	labor	1507	rough	2019	wisdom
484	detect	996	ladder	1508	round	2020	wise
485	develop	997	lady	1509	route	2021	wish
486	device	998	lake	1510	royal	2022	witness
487	devote	999	lamp	1511	rubber	2023	wolf
488	diagram	1000	language	1512	rude	2024	woman
489	dial	1001	laptop	1513	rug	2025	wonder
490	diamond	1002	large	1514	rule	2026	wood
491	diary	1003	later	1515	run	2027	wool
492	dice	1004	latin	1516	runway	2028	word
493	diesel	1005	laugh	1517	rural	2029	work
494	diet	1006	laundry	1518	sad	2030	world
495	differ	1007	lava	1519	saddle	2031	worry
496	digital	1008	law	1520	sadness	2032	worth
497	dignity	1009	lawn	1521	safe	2033	wrap
498	dilemma	1010	lawsuit	1522	sail	2034	wreck
499	dinner	1011	layer	1523	salad	2035	wrestle
500	dinosaur	1012	lazy	1524	salmon	2036	wrist
501	direct	1013	leader	1525	salon	2037	write
502	dirt	1014	leaf	1526	salt	2038	wrong
503	disagree	1015	learn	1527	salute	2039	yard
504	discover	1016	leave	1528	same	2040	year
505	disease	1017	lecture	1529	sample	2041	yellow
506	dish	1018	left	1530	sand	2042	you
507	dismiss	1019	leg	1531	satisfy	2043	young
508	disorder	1020	legal	1532	satoshi	2044	youth
509	display	1021	legend	1533	sauce	2045	zebra
510	distance	1022	leisure	1534	sausage	2046	zero
511	divert	1023	lemon	1535	save	2047	zone
512	divide	1024	lend	1536	say	2048	zoo

KEYS

∞
∞
∞
∞
∞
∞
∞
∞
∞
∞
∞
∞

∞
∞
∞
∞
∞
∞
∞
∞
∞
∞
∞
∞

∞
∞
∞
∞
∞
∞
∞
∞
∞
∞
∞
∞

∞
∞
∞
∞
∞
∞
∞
∞
∞
∞
∞
∞

KEYS

∞	∞
∞	∞
∞	∞
∞	∞
∞	∞
∞	∞
∞	∞
∞	∞
∞	∞
∞	∞
∞	∞
∞	∞

∞	∞
∞	∞
∞	∞
∞	∞
∞	∞
∞	∞
∞	∞
∞	∞
∞	∞
∞	∞
∞	∞
∞	∞

LESSONS LEARNED

+ - Δ

"The meaning of life is to find your gift.
The purpose of life is to give it away." - Pablo Picasso

Made in United States
Troutdale, OR
11/03/2026

56844527R00126